50 JUICIEST BIBLE STORIES

50 JUICIEST BIBLE STORIES

Andy Robb

CWR

Copyright © Andy Robb, 2013
Published 2013 by CWR, Waverley Abbey House, Waverley Lane, Farnham, Surrey GU9 8EP, UK. Registered Charity No. 294387. Registered Limited Company No. 1990308.
The right of Andy Robb to be identified as the author of this work has been asserted by him in accordance with the Copyright, Designs and Patents Act 1988.
All rights reserved. No part of this publication may be reproduced, stored in a retrieval system, or transmitted, in any form or by any means, electronic, mechanical, photocopying, recording or otherwise, without the prior permission in writing of CWR.
See back of book for list of National Distributors.
Unless otherwise indicated, all Scripture references are from the Good News Bible: Old Testament © American Bible Society 1976, 1992; New Testament © American Bible Society 1966, 1971, 1976, 1992
Concept development, editing, design and production by CWR
Cover image: Andy Robb
Printed in China by 1010
ISBN: 978-1-85345-984-9

Intro

Congratulations!

Buying this book is one of the smartest decisions you'll ever make if you're wanting to get your teeth into the Bible but aren't quite sure where to start. Not only have we hand-picked some of the best bits for you, but we've also chopped them up into nice, easy-to-chomp morsels. How's that for thoughtfulness?

In this tasty book we've served up fifty juicy, bite-sized bits of the Bible to munch on and loads of crazy cartoon pics to make them easy for you to digest.

To keep you on your toes, we've mixed up the Old and New Testament stories. Not sure what the difference is between them? It's simple. New Testament stories kick off from when Jesus showed up on planet Earth. The Old Testament happened before that and goes right back to the beginning of time.

But if you're thinking that this book is all about being spoon-fed stuff from the Bible so that you don't have to lift a finger, think again!

At the end of each Bible bit there's some investigating work for you to do, which means you'll need to get your hands on a Bible if you want to find out how the stories end.

Just in case you've bought this book but you don't know much about the Bible, let me give you some useful facts …

Fact number one:

Although the Bible is one book (and what a whopper it is), it's actually made up of sixty-six mini books.

Fact number two:

The Bible wasn't written by just one person like most books. It has over forty authors.

Fact number three:

The Bible was written over a period of roughly 1,500 years.

Fact number four:

Everything that's in the Bible was God's idea.

Next up, you're gonna need to know how to read the Bible – and I don't mean from left to right and top to bottom.

The first thing to know is that every Bible book has got its own name, such as Joshua, Judges, Job, Jeremiah, Joel, Jonah, John, James or Jude. To make these Bible books easier to read, they're handily divided up into chapters (like normal books)

and then each chapter is broken up into verses (like you get in poems). All clear so far? Good!

So, if you wanted to check out Bible book Genesis, chapter 5 and verses 25 to 27, here's how it's often written down:

Genesis 5:25-27

Check out these verses and you'll discover who the world's oldest man was (ever) and how many birthday cards he would have received if they'd been invented way back then (which they hadn't).

That's about it.

So what are you waiting for? Tuck in!

GARDEN GATE GUARD

I don't know if you've got a garden or not but most gardens have some sort of gate to stop people walking in and trampling all over their nice, pretty flower beds or nicking the produce from their vegetable patch. But did you know that the world's very first people (Adam and Eve) had a garden? Yep, they did. Just in case you run away with the idea it had a neat lawn and a stone path leading up to a shed then let me put you straight.

Their garden was the most wonderful, exotic paradise you could ever imagine and four rivers flowed out from it in different directions. Slap-bang in the middle of the garden stood a couple of rather important trees that had been put there by God. Well, actually God had put all the trees there (because He had made the world) but these particular trees were there for a special reason. One of the trees gave life and God had given Adam and Eve the thumbs-up to eat its fruit. The other tree gave the power to know the difference between right and wrong but this one was well and truly off-limits. Take a munch from the fruit of this tree and they were doomed to die. Why spoil things by disobeying God? It was a no-brainer or so you'd have thought.

Just when everything in the garden was looking rosy, along came someone to put a spanner in the works. It was none

other than God's enemy (the devil) masquerading as a sneaky serpent. He'd come to trick the perfect pair into throwing their good life away in a moment of madness. The serpent quickly persuaded them that they'd maybe got the story wrong and that they wouldn't really die if they snacked on some of the forbidden fruit. What could possibly be the harm in just a teensy nibble of the juicy fruit?

So that's exactly what Adam and Eve did. No prizes for guessing that they were rumbled by God. Didn't they know that God doesn't miss a thing? He knew full well that they'd disobeyed Him and now it was time for the consequences. Did God make them mow the lawn or pick up all the leaves as a punishment? Nope, far worse.

Want to find out how this sorry tale ends?

Head for Bible book Genesis, chapter 3 and verses 22 to 24.

2
RAVEN MAD

Right near the beginning of the Bible there's a story about a huge flood that covered the world. It was such a whopper that even the mountain tops were under water. The only people who survived this catastrophe were a chap called Noah and his family. Oh yes, there were some animals that escaped as well. God had told Noah to build a mahoosive box-shaped boat (called an ark) which he filled with pairs of every type of creature you could think of. Anyway, the torrential rain lashed it down for forty days until the only survivors were those on board the ark.

It was obvious that Noah and his fellow passengers couldn't bob up and down on the ocean forever, but how on earth was all that water going to disappear? Was there a plug that God could pull and it would all glug away? Well, sort of. The flood hadn't only been caused by the heavy rain. God had also opened up the Earth's vast underground lakes of water and now God made it drain away, back to where it came from. And to dry things up God sent a rather handy strong breeze. How kind!

After a year or so at sea Noah was keen to put his feet on dry land so he opened a window and let loose a raven to see if it could find any. Annoyingly the runaway raven never returned, which was a fat lot of good. Time for Plan B. Next up Noah sent out a dove. Before long the dove was back. There was no land for it to settle on yet. A week later the dove was dispatched again and this time it came back with an olive tree leaf in its beak. Things were looking up. Another week passed and once again the dove was sent out to look for dry land. Did it find it?

3
WONDER WIFE

I magine having to pack your bags and up sticks to go and live in a foreign land at the age of 65. That's the age when lots of people think about putting their feet up and retiring. But not so for the wife of a chap called Abraham. Sarah and her hubbie had been living the good life in a place called Ur (in Babylon) when God told them to head for the distant land of Canaan where they were going to kick-start a brand new nation of people (the Jews) who would love and worship Him.

Abraham (who was even older than Sarah) promptly obeyed God and the past-it pair eventually rocked up in Canaan along with their family, flocks and servants. According to the Bible, Sarah was looking good for her age and Abraham had his work cut out keeping her from being nabbed by the kings of Canaan because of her beauty. The one small problem with God's plan for Abraham and Sarah to birth a new nation was that they didn't have kids. Not only that but, between you and me, at their ripe old age it hardly seemed likely that they ever would.

After ten years in Canaan with the clock ticking and no baby in sight, Abraham and Sarah decided to take matters into their own hands and Abraham had a son (Ishmael) by Sarah's maidservant (Hagar). Was Ishmael the son and heir through whom the Jewish nation would be birthed? 'Fraid not! Abraham and Sarah had to wait another fourteen years to be told by God that the son He had promised them would finally be born. Oh my days! Sarah was nearly 90 and she laughed out loud at the very thought of it. She wasn't laughing one year later when she gave birth to their son Isaac.

If you want to know how old Sarah was when she finally popped her clogs (died) here's what you'll need to do.

4
FEUDING FAMILY

The guy who heads up this Bible story didn't just do a runner once in his life but twice. First off he had to make a quick exit from his family home (in Canaan) after tricking his twin brother Esau out of his rightful inheritance as the oldest son, and now we catch up with him as he's about to scarper from his father-in-law Laban.

To be fair to Jacob, he'd sort of mended his ways and waved goodbye to being a cheat. For twenty years he'd been working for his Uncle Laban in a place called Haran and had made a pretty good job of it. Along the way Jacob had got himself hitched (married) to Laban's daughters Leah and Rachel (although Rachel was the only one of the two he'd really wanted to wed) and as a result he had produced twelve kids. Okay, so his wives' maidservants also had a part to play in this but that's another story.

Jacob looked after Laban's flocks and because God was looking after Jacob the size of the flock just grew and grew and grew. Did Laban appreciate his son-in-law's efforts? No way. Laban was a nasty piece of work and was out for all he could get from Jacob. So when Jacob was told by God to pack his bags and head back home to Canaan, our main man decided

to ask his father-in-law for some sheep and goats to take with him. Seems like a reasonable request. Not to Laban. He did his level best to trick Jacob out of having anything.

God scuppered Laban's scheming ways and with enough sheep and goats to begin his new life Jacob was ready to roll. Did Laban throw a big farewell party for his hardworking son-in-law?

All is revealed in Bible book Genesis, chapter 31 and verses 4 to 18.

5
SON RISE

This Bible story stars a dad who hadn't seen his long-lost son for twenty-two tearful years. His name was Jacob and his son Joseph was the apple of his eye (which is another way of saying that Joseph was his favourite).

Unsurprisingly, that didn't really go down too well with Joseph's other eleven brothers and the long and the short of it was that they sold Joseph into slavery and he ended up in the land of Egypt. As far as Jacob was concerned, Joseph had been killed by a wild animal. That's the story his other sons told their distraught dad. But this sorry tale doesn't end there because God had big plans for Joseph's life and after a few ups and downs (such as being chucked into prison for something he didn't do) Joseph ended up as the right-hand man of Egypt's powerful ruler (Pharaoh). Not bad going for a Hebrew slave.

When a famine hit the region Joseph's brothers turned up, cap in hand, begging for food. They'd absolutely no idea that it was their brother Joseph whom they were grovelling to but *he* certainly recognised *them*. Joseph eventually came clean and owned up about who he was. No surprise that the brothers were scared witless that Joseph would have their guts for garters and get his revenge for their dastardly deed all those years ago.

But Joseph had other plans. Not only did he let bygones be bygones but he made sure that his brothers came to live in Egypt during the famine. More than that, he wanted to be reunited with his dear old dad. Jacob couldn't believe his eyes when he was brought face to face with the son he thought was dead. Egypt's Pharaoh welcomed Joseph's family with open arms and gave them tip-top grazing land for their flocks in a place called Goshen.

Jacob could finally die a happy man. He did actually return to the land he'd come from, but not in quite the way you'd expect.

You've probably heard of a fella called Moses, haven't you? Well, this Bible bit is all about his father-in-law, Jethro. Moses had been looking after Jethro's flocks before God had sent him to Egypt to set free all its Israelite slaves. Now with his mission accomplished, Moses was leading the Israelites to a land in which to settle.

Between you and me, things hadn't been going too well and the Israelites were giving Moses a bit of a hard time. You'd think they'd be pleased that they weren't slaves any more, but the novelty of it was quickly wearing off. Trudging through the hot desert was no fun and they were beginning to wish that they were back in Egypt. Okay, so it was tough there but at least they had a roof over their heads and plenty of food and water. What a bunch of moaners and groaners they were.

Jethro got wind of the fact that Moses was heading his way and decided to go out and meet his son-in-law. The pair of them had a great old catch up time and Moses filled Jethro in with how God had sent plague after plague on the Egyptians until they finally gave in and let their slaves go free.

Someone has worked out that there were probably somewhere between two and three million Israelites who escaped from Egypt, so that was a lot of people that Moses had to lead, as Jethro soon discovered. The very next morning Moses was back to work. One by one, people brought their complaints to him and one by one, Moses sorted them out. It seemed never ending. Moses would be worn to a frazzle if he carried on like this, and Jethro knew it.

Jethro had an idea to make leading the Israelites less of a stress.

TIP TOP TENT

I f you've ordered this book online then one thing's for sure - the people you bought it from needed to know where you live so that they could mail it to you. In the Old Testament bit of the Bible there was a place called the Tabernacle tent and that was where God lived.

Okay, so we all know that God lives in heaven, but because He's God He can also live in a tent if He wants to. The tent we're talking about was no ordinary tent. It was the place where the Israelites' leader met with God and it was where handpicked men called priests made special sacrifices to God. In fact, it was so special that everything about it was designed by God Himself. He'd given the Israelites' leader (Moses) the instructions for what it should look like down to the very last detail. Not only was the outside just as God wanted it but so was the inside. Everything had to be done perfectly and beautifully so it reflected what things were like in heaven.

To make sure that His instructions were carried out to the letter, God chose a couple of super-duper craftsmen called Bezalel and Oholiab to run the show. Making a tent for God with gold covered furniture and the finest fixtures and fittings

didn't come cheap. The Israelites clubbed together until Moses was so stashed with cash he had to call a halt to their giving.

Was God chuffed with the Tabernacle tent and was He happy to live in it?

Here's where you'll find the answer to that question. Bible book Exodus, chapter 40 and verses 34 to 38.

8
KING CAPERS

After many years of being just one nation, Israel did the splits and became two nations. The south of the land became known as Judah and the north kept the name of Israel. All in all, Judah did a better job than Israel of following their God but both had their fair share of bad kings.

One of Judah's rotten rulers was Jehoiakim. Time and time again God had sent prophets to warn His people to turn from their wicked ways but time and time again they'd dug their heels in and ignored God. God wasn't planning to stand by and watch the nation that He'd started (to show people what He was like) make such a terrible hash of things. God was calling time on their disobedience by allowing the Babylonians to come in and conquer them. One by one, the towns of Judah were attacked and destroyed but still the people refused to mend their ways.

Just when things were hotting up, King Jehoiakim of Judah died leaving his young son Jehoiachin to take the reins of reigning. Let's be honest, it wasn't the best time to succeed to the throne, right in the middle of an enemy invasion. According to the Bible Jehoiachin was a chip off the old block and was as bad as his dad. Jehoiachin didn't have long to get used to the idea of being Judah's ruler. Just three months later, Nebuchadezzar (Babylon's king) sent his troops to attack Judah's capital city, Jerusalem. The new king didn't put up a fight but simply surrendered to the Babylonians. He knew that the game was up and he didn't stand a chance. King Jehoiachin was captured along with the royal household and taken into captivity in Babylon.

9

WAY TO PRAY

Here's a question for you. How should you pray? It's not just 'hands together and close your eyes'. That's only to help you concentrate and so you don't get distracted. I mean what sort of things should you talk to God about when you pray to Him?

While you're pondering that, let me tell you about the time when Jesus' disciples asked their Master the very same thing. Jesus had been doing a spot of praying Himself and when He'd wrapped up, one of His disciples said, 'Lord, teach us to pray'. What Jesus came up with has become known as 'The Lord's Prayer' and it's been used by people from then until now as a prayer to God. But interestingly enough, the chap wasn't actually asking Jesus *what* to pray. He was asking *how* to pray, which is a very different thing.

The prayer Jesus taught His disciples was like a pattern that we could use each time we talk to God. So, here's what Jesus suggested. First off, how about beginning by focusing on God and not just on what we need from Him. Next up, pray that all the good things that are in heaven are brought down to earth. *Then* it's time to bring to God your needs such as for food, for health, for friends, for whatever. We can also ask God to forgive us for the things we've done wrong at the same time as making sure we let people off the hook who have wronged us.

And finally we can pray for God to help us live lives that make Him happy and so we don't do stuff that displeases Him. Jesus added one last little bit at the end that's worth checking out to make sure our prayers do get answered.

PRACTICE MAKES PERFECT

Jesus had hand-picked a hotchpotch bunch of twelve men (His disciples) whom He was going to train up to carry on from Him once He'd returned to heaven. Jesus was on a mission to get people back to being friends with God and not only was Jesus going to show His disciples how to do this, but He was going to give them the power to back it up as well.

If you check out the Bible bits about Jesus you'll soon see that He gave His trusty band of followers plenty of opportunity to practise what they were being taught. All the way through, Jesus kept encouraging them to think big and to expect God to do great things. One time Jesus gave them the chance to feed 5,000 people with little more than a young lad's packed lunch. They flunked it and Jesus had to step in to do the miracle. Another time they were on a boat with Jesus when a storm blew up. The disciples were petrified so Jesus had to command the storm to stop, and it did. But Jesus left them in no doubt that they could have stopped the storm if they'd trusted in God a bit more.

Over time, the penny began to drop that Jesus had given them the authority to do the same stuff as He was doing. One day, as if to prove His point, Jesus got the twelve together, gave them a pep talk and sent them off to put into practice what they'd learned. Jesus instructed them to head for the Jewish towns and villages and to tell the inhabitants that Jesus was the special person (or Messiah) sent by God that their traditions spoke of.

But one last thing. If the Jewish people they talked to rejected Jesus as their Messiah, Jesus told His disciples to do something rather odd.

MICKEY-TAKING MOCKERS

Y ou'd have thought that everyone would have liked Jesus because of the love He showed to people and because of the healing miracles He performed, but no. Maybe the reason some people hated Him so much was because Jesus never put a foot wrong and that made them feel uneasy about how bad they were. Who knows?

But what we *do* know is that Jesus had plenty of enemies when He lived on earth and none more so than the religious leaders who resented His popularity. After loads of failed attempts they finally managed to have Jesus arrested on a trumped-up charge. With Jesus held captive they wasted no time in giving Him a hard time. In fact everyone now seemed to have it in for Jesus. As He waited to be put on trial in front of the Jewish high priest, His guards blindfolded Him, beat Him round the head and taunted Him. Jesus was then put on trial in front of the Roman governor (Pontius Pilate). The Roman soldiers guarding Jesus took great delight in making Him a laughing stock by dressing Him up as a king and then beating Him.

Finally, Jesus was nailed to a wooden cross and left to die, but even there the mocking continued. Passers-by yelled abuse at Him daring Him to prove that He was God by coming down off the cross. Not to be outdone, the religious leaders also seized the chance to take the mickey out of God's Son. 'He saved others, but He cannot save himself.'

When Jesus died and a mighty earthquake rocked the region not everyone was quite so quick to mock Jesus.

PRUNE JEWS

id you know that you're more likely to remember something you've been told if there's a picture with it? That's the reason this book has cartoons. Jesus also knew all about using pictures to help people to remember things, which is why He used everyday objects to illustrate the stories He told about God.

When Jesus knew that His time on earth was nearly done He took His disciples to one side and told them how they could be successful in life. In Israel (where Jesus lived) it was generally very warm which meant that things like grapes grew really well. Jesus decided to teach His trusty band of followers some important lessons about being a Christian using a grape vine as a handy visual aid. For starters Jesus likened Himself to the vine. Without Him they wouldn't be able to bear any fruit (which is another of way of saying they wouldn't be able to be successful followers of Jesus).

Jesus then said that the Jewish people were like the branches that grew out from the vine. The Jewish people were meant to be fruitful for God. If you know anything at all about gardening you'll know that plants need pruning (cutting back and trimming) every now and then to make

them produce even more fruit. So not only was it mega important that they stayed rooted in Jesus, it was also important that they were regularly pruned.

Wow! What an easy way to remember that if we stay connected to Jesus we not only grow as Christians but we can be effective in helping other people know that God loves them as well.

Want to know who'll do the pruning Jesus spoke about?

You'll find your answer in Bible book John, chapter 15 and verses 1 and 2.

13
ALIVE AND KICKING

If you know anything at all about Jesus there's a pretty good chance you know that He was nailed to a wooden cross by the Roman rulers of Israel and left to die. Between you and me, it was the Jewish religious leaders who'd been behind the whole thing and as far as they were concerned it was good riddance! Jesus had criticised them for doing a bad job of heading up the Jewish religion and they figured they'd finally seen the last of Him.

Not so. What they *hadn't* got their heads round was that Jesus was God's Son. That meant that God wasn't going to let Jesus rot in a tomb somewhere, never to be seen again. God had other ideas. Jesus had come to earth to take the punishment (the death penalty) for all the wrong things people do. That's what He did on the cross. It was now job done and time to return to heaven. So God brought Jesus back to life again with a new heaven-and-earth type body which could appear and disappear at the drop of a hat.

To prove He was alive and kicking Jesus appeared to loads and loads of His followers over a period of forty days. The first people He showed up to were a couple of His female followers who'd gone to Jesus' tomb to pay their respects. He also rocked

up to a couple of His disciples as they were on their way to the town of Emmaus. They hadn't the foggiest idea that it was Jesus who'd joined them for the journey until they arrived at their destination and with that He simply disappeared. They promptly turned on their heels and headed straight back to Jerusalem to tell the other disciples about their amazing encounter. In the middle of all this, Jesus suddenly appeared to the lot of 'em.

Arrgh! It was a ghost! Or was it?

Find out in Bible book Luke chapter 24 and verses 38 to 43.

14
WATER STRANGE STORY

There are a few stories in the Bible about people crossing stretches of water in odd and unconventional ways, and we're not talking about using jet skis, building a suspension bridge or doing the backstroke. Let me give you some examples.

For instance, there was the time when the Israelite nation needed to get from one side of the River Jordan to the other. To make matters worse, it was flood season and it looked like there was absolutely no chance of getting across. It might have seemed impossible for them but it was no problem for God. He simply held the water back upstream and over they went.

Then there was the time that Jesus walked across the Sea of Galilee in the middle of the night to catch up with His disciples who were rowing across. And not forgetting that well-known story about the Israelite nation escaping from slavery in Egypt. Having got their marching orders from Egypt's Pharaoh, they'd found themselves at the banks of the Red Sea with no way of getting to the other side. It didn't help that Pharaoh had changed his mind and had sent his army to recapture the Israelites. Just when the Israelites thought that all was lost, God told their leader (Moses) to hold out his wooden staff over the sea and He would open up a pathway over which they could cross to the other side. Sure enough, the Israelites got across but the Egyptians weren't so fortunate. They were all drowned when the waters closed back over them as they followed in hot pursuit.

But there's one more rather odd story that I think you'll find fascinating. It features two prophets called Elijah and Elisha and we catch up with them as they are about to cross a river in an extraordinary way.

15

MEGA MESSENGERS

Throughout the Old Testament part of the Bible, people called prophets keep popping up. Their job was to take time out to listen to what God was saying and then pass the message on to whoever God wanted to hear it. These prophets show up all through the history of God's special nation, Israel.

Isaiah, Jeremiah and Ezekiel were three fellas who got the nickname 'major prophets', not because they were any better than the others, but simply because they had so much to say. You'll have probably worked out that the rest of them were called the 'minor prophets'. Anyway, it's Isaiah we've picked out for this odd Bible bit.

Isaiah has a whopping sixty-six chapters to his name in the Bible (which, coincidentally, is the same number of books that there are in the Bible). Someone has also calculated that this prolific prophet delivered his messages from God for around sixty-four years. That's roughly one chapter for every year that he was a prophet. One of Isaiah's claims to fame was predicting how Jesus would be born. Isaiah was also spot-on about where Jesus would live and work, how His life would end and where He'd be buried. And this was over seven hundred years before it all happened. Wow!

Being a prophet of God wasn't something any Tom, Dick or Harry could do. It also wasn't the sort of job which you had to apply for. To be a prophet you had to be handpicked by God. That's the way it happened for Isaiah. Isaiah had been minding his own business when he suddenly found himself seeing all sorts of weird and wonderful things in his head. The Bible calls these visions. It was like he was in heaven (where God lives) and he was able to see God in all His power and awesomeness.

Poor Isaiah was a bit overwhelmed by it all. How could someone perfect like God use someone like him who was so imperfect? God had already thought of that.

16

PILATE IN A PICKLE

magine getting blamed for something you didn't do. It's annoying, isn't it? That's exactly what happened to Jesus towards the end of His life. For over three years Jesus had criss-crossed Israel telling people about God and demonstrating how much God loved them by healing them of their sickness. All in all, Jesus was a popular guy with the crowds. Okay, so the religious leaders weren't too fond of Him because of the way He pointed out their failings and because He seemed to undermine their authority but on the whole, Jesus was a hit with the people.

To cut a long story short, Jesus found Himself on trial before the Roman governor (a chap called Pontius Pilate) accused of breaking the Jewish law. It had been a set-up job by the religious leaders to get rid of Jesus any way they could. It was a bit of a tricky one for Pontius Pilate. He couldn't really make head or tail of what Jesus was being accused of and as far as he was concerned, Jesus was innocent. Even Pilate's wife got in on the act and tried to persuade her hubbie (after having a dream about Jesus) to let Him off.

The harder the governor tried to let Jesus loose, the more the religious leaders stirred things up. Pilate had a brain wave.

Once a year at the Jewish Passover festival (which it was right then) they had a custom where a person of their choice could be let off the death penalty. The Roman governor figured that it was a no-brainer. Jesus was guilty of nothing. The crowds seemed to love Him. They'd pick Jesus to be set free and his troubles would be over. What Pilate hadn't bargained on was the religious leaders stirring up the crowds.

Want to find out the result of their dirty work?

Head for Bible book Mark, chapter 15 and verses 8 to 15.

17
MAT MATES

The New Testament part of the Bible is full of stories of how Jesus healed people of all kinds of sicknesses and ailments. There weren't hospitals and qualified doctors in those days, so it was hit and miss if you got better or not.

Jesus had come from heaven to earth with the power and authority to make people well again as a sign of God's love. Word soon got out that Jesus could heal people and before long He was attracting large crowds wanting Him to make them better. Often it seemed that just a touch from Jesus would release the power to heal someone.

One time a sick lady squeezed through a crowd that was swamping Jesus just so that she could touch the hem of His garment. As soon as she touched it she was healed. Jesus knew that something had happened and told the lady that she'd got her healing because she'd had faith in His power to heal. Another time, as Jesus and His disciples were out and about a blind man (called Bartimaeus) yelled out to Jesus to heal him. The poor chap was desperate and Jesus was his only hope. Bartimaeus didn't leave disappointed and his eyesight was completely restored.

The peculiar Bible story I'm going to tell you next is all about a sick man who also desperately needed a healing touch from Jesus but there were some big obstacles to overcome first. For starters, the man was bed-bound so there was no way that he was going to get to Jesus on foot. So his mates carried their poorly pal all the way to Jesus on a mat. So far, so good. On their arrival at the house where Jesus was staying it soon become clear that there was a fat chance of getting anywhere near Him. The place was heaving with people.

What they did next was more than a little unusual but, as you'll see, it did the job.

Check out Bible book Mark, chapter 2 and verses 3 to 12.

POOPED PROPHET

Elijah was an awesome man of God and there's no way that you'd have wanted to mess with this powerful prophet. Elijah was fearless and didn't mind telling people when they were out of line with God. That didn't make things easy for him, especially when I tell you that the king of Israel (where Elijah lived) was a bad 'un. In fact so was his wife.

Their names were Ahab and Jezebel and they didn't like Elijah one little bit. He was forever pointing out how they'd turned their backs on Israel's God to go and worship the gods of other nations. Elijah had just had a bit of a showdown with this pair of rotten rulers which ended up with hundreds of Jezebel's prophets getting slaughtered. She was not a happy bunny. Grrr! Jezebel wanted Elijah's guts for garters, which is another way of saying she wanted him dead.

The power-packed prophet was suddenly petrified and did a runner as far from the furious queen as his legs would take him. Elijah then plonked himself down under a bush and decided that he'd had enough of this being a prophet malarkey. Between you and me, I think the poor fella was feeling a bit sorry for himself. Then God suddenly showed up and asked the pooped prophet why he was throwing in the towel.

Elijah gave God a sob story about how it was just him against the whole world and that he'd had enough.

Right, time to remind Elijah that although he might have felt alone God was always with him, but not always in the ways he might expect. God told Elijah to stand in a mountain cave and He'd show up as a reminder to Elijah that he wasn't alone. Suddenly a wild wind shook the mountain, but nope, that wasn't God. Then there was an earthquake that rocked the mountain, but still that wasn't God. Next up fire blazed all around. Was God in it? Nope again.

Want to find out how God revealed Himself to Elijah?

Look up Bible book 1 Kings, chapter 19 and verses 12 and 13.

19
DONKEY DUMPED

I don't know about you, but I really like Christmas. The story of Jesus' mum and dad travelling to Bethlehem on a donkey is retold every year at countless Christmas nativities. I'm sorry to burst your bubble, but the Bible doesn't actually say that Mary rode to Bethlehem on a donkey (although it does sound like a comfy way for a pregnant mum to travel doesn't it?). Because Jesus' dad was only a lowly carpenter the chances are that their budget probably couldn't stretch to owning a donkey (unless, of course, somebody had lent them one, but we'll never know).

Anyway, don't be too sad. Jesus might not have got His donkey ride as a baby, but He most certainly got it as an adult. Let me fill you in. Jesus was making tracks for Jerusalem (Israel's capital city) where He knew that He'd meet His end. The Jewish religious leaders had had enough of Jesus and were baying for His blood. Jesus knew that before very long they'd get their wish and God's one and only Son would be killed.

As Jesus and His disciples approached the outskirts of Jerusalem, He sent a couple of them off to one of the villages to fetch a donkey. Jesus mounted the donkey and off they headed for Jesus' final showdown in the city. Crowds of people lined the route and flung their cloaks or the branches of palm trees on the ground in front of Him. Everyone was whooping and cheering for Jesus. The religious leaders might have had it in for Him but not the ordinary people. They loved Him. Little did they know how things would end.

A guy called Paul crops up an awful lot in the New Testament part of the Bible. In fact, Paul even wrote huge chunks of it. Paul was quite a character and having had his life turned round by Jesus, he wanted to tell the world about it. Not everyone was happy with the way Paul had changed. He started out as a Jewish religious leader who had it in for followers of Jesus and now he was a follower of Jesus himself. Paul was more than a little outspoken and often as not he found himself in hot water because of this.

This Bible story is all about how Paul found himself in *cold* water (for a change). Because the religious leaders weren't too fond of him, Paul had been banged up in prison. He hadn't done anything wrong, other than getting up their noses, which was jolly unfair don't you think? Well, Paul thought so. Being a Roman citizen he decided to demand a fair trial in front of the Roman emperor (called Caesar). That meant a long, long journey to Rome and because aeroplanes hadn't been invented yet, there was nothing for it but to go by sea and over land. With winter on the way it wasn't really the best time of the year to be setting sail.

They had setback after setback until the ship finally docked at the island of Crete and the crew resigned themselves to spending the winter there. The harbour they'd ended up in wasn't really ideal so the ship's captain decided to chance it and sail round the island to find somewhere better. Big mistake! A whopper of a wind blew the ship out to sea and for fourteen terrifying days they were at the mercy of the elements.

Did Paul live to tell the tale?

21
JADED JUDAS

When Jesus handpicked his twelve disciples (the guys who went everywhere with Him for over three years) He knew full well that one of them was going to do the dirty on Him and would one day betray Him. Judas was the guy in question.

The Bible says that he was their treasurer and held the purse strings. Jesus and His followers couldn't live on fresh air so they would have needed money (perhaps gifts from friends) and Judas took care of it for them. Who knows what was going through the mind of Judas as he watched Jesus teach people about God and heal the sick? There wasn't a bad bone in Jesus' body, so why on earth would Judas want to turn his back on the man God had sent to rescue us?

Although God had sent Jesus down to earth (from heaven) to patch things up between us and God maybe Judas had other ideas. Perhaps Judas thought that if Jesus was God's Son (which He was) shouldn't He be doing something about getting rid of the rotten Romans who had invaded their country? Whatever Judas was thinking, the bottom line was that the religious leaders were looking for a way to arrest Jesus and Judas was up for helping them.

No matter which way you look at it, Judas finally gave up on Jesus and for thirty pieces of silver he offered to tell Jesus' enemies where they could nab Him, away from the adoring crowds who hung on His every word.

I wonder if Judas regretted doing such a rash thing?

Find out the answer in Bible book Matthew, chapter 27 and verses 3 to 5.

22

RULER RUMPUS

All through the Bible you can read stories that show us what God is like, how He wants us to live and the brilliant life He's got lined up for anyone who makes Him No.1 in their life.

The nation of Israel had been set up by God to do just that. The trouble was that the Israelites were a tough nut to crack and they were forever wanting to do things their way and not God's way. On more than one occasion God went so far as to call them a 'stiff-necked people', which wasn't a compliment by the way.

Early on in their history they'd had some great leaders like Abraham and Moses but that wasn't God's long-term plan for His special nation. God wanted to lead them Himself. When they'd lived in the desert, God had lived among them in a tent called the Tabernacle. It was a sort of visual aid of how God wanted things to be; a nation who had Him at the centre of everything.

Eventually the Israelites settled down in the land of Canaan and God gave them leaders called judges to rule over them. When the final judge had breathed his last, a guy called Samuel stepped up to the plate and held the reins of Israel for a while. But when it looked like Samuel's days were numbered the Israelites weren't too keen on Samuel's sons taking over.

Joel and Abijah were a couple of crooks and the people of Israel didn't want them running the show.

Actually what they now wanted was a king. All the other nations had one, so why couldn't they? God was none too pleased about this. It seemed like the idea of God being the One who was going to lead them had gone out of the window. God did give the Israelites a king but not before warning them of the consequences.

GOODBYE GOODIES

For hundreds of years the Israelite nation had been held captive in Egypt where they'd worked as slaves. It had been gruelling and tough but during that time God's special nation had grown and grown into the millions.

The Egyptians were getting a bit nervous about this and were worried that the Israelites might revolt and overthrow them. So the Egyptian slave drivers worked the Israelites into the ground to prevent them rising up. The good news is that God was on their case and sent a guy called Moses to set them free from their terrible plight. That said, it wasn't quite as straightforward as they might have liked. Egypt's Pharaoh (their ruler) wasn't too happy about losing his free workforce which he was using to build bigger and better cities. He dug his heels in and refused to let them leave. God responded by sending one destructive plague after another until Pharaoh finally relented and let the Israelites go.

You'd have thought that plagues of crop-destroying locusts or body-covering boils would have done the trick but it took the death of every firstborn Egyptian human and animal to make Pharaoh loosen his grip and to tell Moses to take the Israelites and scram.

But here's the thing. God had given the Israelites a heads-up they were leaving sharpish and instructed them to knock on the doors of their Egyptian neighbours beforehand. Was it so they could say cheerio? It wasn't. It was to ask the Egyptians to give them gold, silver and clothes to start their new life. Was that going to work? I'd have thought that the Egyptians would have been well cheesed-off with the trouble-making Israelites and slammed the door in their faces. Did they?

24
GOBBLEDEGOOK GONE

Someone has worked out that there could be up to 7,000 different languages in the world. Wow! That said, some of them aren't spoken by more than a few hundred people, unlike Mandarin which is inching up towards a billion users. Double wow! So how come there are all these languages in the first place? Wouldn't it have been easier for us all if God had just created one language for everyone to speak? That way we'd be able to talk to people all over the globe without using phrase books or having to learn other languages at school.

For your information, that's just how things were when God created the world. Nobody has a clue what that language was or what it sounded like but there was just the one language. The reason there are up to 7,000 different ones now is all down to our distant ancestors. God had given them strict instructions to populate the entire world. Unfortunately they chose to do their own thing and settle down in a region called Babylonia and to go no further. To make matters worse they also decided that they didn't really need God any more. They could manage quite well on their own, thank you very much. God was having none of it and swiftly scuppered their plans by mixing things up so that instead of all just speaking the one language they now spoke loads of different languages. How confusing was that?

There was nothing for it but for those who spoke one language to live in one place (so they could understand each other) and for those who spoke another language to live in another place. And that's how God got them moving again and so how they ended up inhabiting the whole world. Neat huh? But many years later, when God wanted people of every language to find out who Jesus was He did something rather unusual to make sure everyone understood.

BAD BUDDIES

At the time of Jesus' birth, Israel was under Roman occupation (which means that it was part of their mahoosive Roman empire) and Israel (or part of it) was ruled by someone called Herod. This wasn't his first name – it was just the name of the family that ruled the region. The Herod that we're homing in on was called Herod Antipas and he was a nasty piece of work let me tell you. I guess he might have felt a wee bit unsettled knowing that the Romans were always breathing down his neck. And being a 'puppet king' (a ruler who has to do what he's told by a higher authority, such as the Romans) was probably a bit degrading.

It was none other than Herod Antipas who'd given the orders to chop off the head of a guy called John the Baptist and then serve it to his wife's daughter on a platter. Not nice! (John the Baptist was a prophet of God who announced to one and all that Jesus was on the way.) So not only wasn't Herod Antipas best buddies with the Roman rulers but he was also a bit of a meanie.

Towards the end of Jesus' life on earth He was brought before the Roman governor (Pontius Pilate) to be put on trial for breaking the Jewish law. Pilate was baffled and when he discovered that Jesus was from Galilee (where Herod ruled) he sent him off to see Antipas. Herod was thrilled. He'd been waiting to meet Jesus and hoped that maybe He could do one of His miracles that He was famous for. Jesus wasn't playing ball and remained tight-lipped throughout the ordeal. All the while Herod, the religious leaders with him and Herod's soldiers taunted and mocked Jesus. When Herod got round to sending Jesus back to Pilate something had changed between the two of them.

King David of Israel had more than his fair share of sons and one of them was called Absalom. The Bible tells us that he was a jolly handsome chap and had luscious, long hair which he had cut once a year. That's got absolutely nothing to do with this story but I thought it might interest you.

Absalom's elder brother (a guy called Amnon) had really riled him big time. He'd treated his half-sister Tamar (and Absalom's full sister) very badly indeed and Absalom was fuming mad. He wanted revenge for what Amnon had done to Tamar and plotted in his heart to kill him. It didn't help matters that Amnon was their dad's blue-eyed boy and could do no wrong as far as he was concerned. If their dad wasn't going to punish Amnon then Absalom decided that he'd have to do it.

Two years passed and Absalom enticed his big, bad brother to a slap-up feast at his house. As soon as he'd got Amnon sozzled (drunk) Absalom's servants seized their chance and killed him. While King David tried to come to terms with the death of his son, Absalom hot-footed it as far away as he could get. One part of David was angry at Absalom but another part of him missed his son-on-the-run. What was he to do?

Joab (David's military commander) had a plan to make the king see sense. He sent a woman in disguise to visit David and to spin him a yarn about one of her sons who'd killed his brother. People wanted the murdering son dead but she appealed to the king to spare his life. King David knew that to lose both sons would be more than she could bear and said that he'd make sure the remaining son lived. The woman then pointed out that this was just like Amnon and Absalom and that the king should have mercy on his living son also. David agreed not to harm even a hair of Absalom's head and commanded Joab to go fetch his runaway son.

The story didn't quite end there. It was a full two years before David could face seeing his son. Want to find out how it all ended?

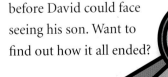

Take a look in Bible book 2 Samuel, chapter 14 and verses 28 to 33.

27
WORST CURSE

Rachel and her sister (Leah) had arrived in the land of Canaan with their hubbie, Jacob (yes, he had two wives!) from the faraway land of Haran where they'd grown up. Rachel and Jacob had fallen head over heels in love with each other, but Rachel's dad was not going to have his oldest daughter left on the shelf and so he sneakily tricked Jacob into marrying Leah first.

Rachel didn't worship the same God as Jacob and so she'd nicked her dad's household idols (that she worshipped) before they'd left for Canaan. This had caused a right old rumpus when Laban (her dad) had found out they were missing. Rachel didn't own up to the fact, but Jacob was livid and cursed whoever was responsible. 'If you find that any one of us has taken your idols, I'll have that person killed,' he promised Laban.

You'd think that a dozen kids would be enough for Jacob, but before long another son was on its way. That would make a grand total of twelve boys and one girl. Pretty impressive, eh? Jacob and Rachel only had one child between them. His name was Joseph. The rest of the children were borne by Leah or their maidservants. Rachel must have been over the moon to be pregnant with another of Jacob's children but things were about to go pear-shaped.

Jacob and his family were heading for a place called Bethel where God had told them to put down roots. If only Rachel hadn't stolen her dad's idols and if only Jacob hadn't pronounced the death sentence on the culprit then what I'm about to tell you might never have happened. As Jacob and his large family made tracks for Bethel, the time came for Rachel to give birth. Sadly, the love of Jacob's life died on the roadside.

TREE TROUBLE

Things weren't good between a guy called Absalom and his dad, King David. Israel's ruler and his son had fallen out and Absalom now had his sights set on taking his dad's crown and becoming king himself.

Day after day, he'd hang out on the road that led up to the city of Jerusalem and would pretend to people (on their way to have their disputes sorted by the king) that David wasn't really interested in them. He sucked up to them and made out that if *he* was running the show he'd be much fairer. Before long everyone loved Absalom. His plan to overthrow his dad was working.

Next up, the scheming son persuaded his dad to let him take a trip to a place called Hebron (along with two hundred of his men). Once there, Absalom declared himself king of Hebron. In no time at all, Absalom had a vast army of supporters from far and wide and now he was ready to head back to Jerusalem to claim the crown. When King David got wind of Absalom's plot to overthrow him he panicked and fled the city with his family and close friends. But the king wasn't prepared to give in quite yet.

He sent his friend Hushai back to Jerusalem to act as his spy. Hushai quickly won the confidence of Absalom and persuaded him to ignore the advice of his personal advisor (Ahithophel) and to go along with his cunning plan for attacking David. It was actually a trick and Hushai was setting Absalom up for defeat. Sure enough Absalom and his fighting men went off in hot pursuit of King David but they soon discovered that they were no match for David's crack troops.

The battle took place in the forest of Ephraim and the Bible says that more people were killed because of injuries due to the forest than through warfare.

29 HAZAEL HAS HIS DAY

There are plenty of people from the Bible that you might have heard of such as Noah, Moses, and Jesus, but my guess is that you've probably not heard of a fella called Hazael. Am I right? If I'm not, then give yourself a pat on the back for being such a smarty pants.

Anyway, Hazael first crops up in Bible book 1 Kings and chapter 19, when God instructs the prophet Elijah to anoint the unsuspecting chap as the next king of Syria (where Elijah lives). God was planning to use Hazael to help rid the region of worship to the horrible god Baal (which meant killing everyone who worshipped Baal). Not the nicest job, eh? If Hazael missed any of them, fear not, God had lined up a guy called Jehu to come to the rescue. If any of the Baal worshippers got away from Jehu then God's backstop was the prophet Elijah himself.

That's all we then hear of Hazael until he pops up again in Bible book 2 Kings, chapter 8. Elijah's successor, Elisha (yes, I know it's confusing that their names sound so similar but it can't be helped) was on his way to Damascus (the capital of Syria) to drop in on the king. No, it wasn't Hazael. Well, not yet anyway.

Although Elijah had anointed Hazael king, his time hadn't yet come. But it was about to.

King Benhadad was on the throne at that point but he was a poorly person. When he found out Elisha was in town he packed off Hazael with a gift for the prophet to make him feel welcome. In case you're wondering, it wasn't a box of chocolates or anything like that. Hazael rocked up with forty camel loads of goodies for Elisha in the hope that the prophet would make his master well again. Sorry, nice try, but no amount of gifts was going to change things. Elisha told Hazael that his master wouldn't recover and that was that.

Want to find out if Elisha was right?

Head off to Bible book 2 Kings, chapter 8 and verses 14 and 15.

MEAN QUEEN

Not only is the Bible jam-packed full of loads of really good guys and gals but it's also got its fair share of bad 'uns. That's because the Bible tells it as it is and doesn't try to make out that people don't make mistakes or do bad stuff.

The Bible baddy we're going to take a look at now was none other than Queen Athaliah of Judah. Her hubby (King Jehoram) had been one of the goodies and was in fact a descendant of King David (who was also, on the whole, a goodie). Sad to say, Queen Athaliah wasn't from such good stock. Her mum and dad were those notorious Bible baddies, King Ahab and Queen Jezebel. Boo!

Jehoram and Athaliah's marriage had been arranged to keep things sweet between the nation of Israel (where Athaliah came from) and the nation of Judah (where Jehoram came from). Athaliah was a bit of a bad influence on Jehoram and persuaded him to allow the worship of her god Baal as well as Judah's God who Jehoram worshipped. After King Jehoram's death their son, Ahaziah was crowned king but he didn't last long in the job. To be honest he was a bit of a chip off the old block and was no better than his mum when it came to being a Bible baddy.

King Ahaziah was killed in battle a year later and Queen Athaliah seized her chance. She figured that now was her time to be centre stage and to rule Judah – but first things first. To make sure that she wasn't ousted from the throne she set about having every descendant of King David (the goodies) put to death. That included any of her grandchildren who were related to King David's family line.

Did anyone escape from her devilish plot?

All is revealed in Bible book 2 Kings, chapter 11 and verses 2 and 3.

SUPER SOLOMON

Did you know that King Solomon was one of the wisest men in the Bible? Well, he was. Solomon was the son of Israel's King David and he had a tough act to follow taking over from his dad as king of God's special nation. Which is why, before he really got off the starting blocks, Solomon asked God for something more important than heaps of gold, loads of power or victory over his enemies.

It all came about when Israel's new king had a dream in which God appeared to him and said that he could ask for anything he wanted and God would give it to him. That's an offer nobody could refuse. Solomon decided that the thing he needed above everything else from God was wisdom and the ability to know what was right and what was wrong. Good call, Solomon! God gave the king wisdom by the bucket load and although Solomon didn't mention anything about silver or gold, God said that because King Solomon had made such a good choice He'd give him great wealth as well.

Solomon didn't have long to wait to have the chance to use his new found wisdom. A couple of ladies appeared at the palace both claiming a baby was theirs. To settle the dispute, King Solomon proposed that the baby be cut in two so they

could have half each. One of the ladies refused to go along with this. She'd rather the other woman keep the child than see it killed. As far as the king was concerned that proved that she was the mum. Only the true mum would do anything she could to protect her child. And she was the one whom Solomon gave the baby to. How wise was that?

King Solomon's wisdom was so amazing that people travelled from far and wide to hear what he had to say. The Queen of Sheba was one such visitor. With her vast entourage in tow, she trekked hundreds of miles just to meet the man himself. And she wasn't disappointed.

Find out what she had to say about her trip in Bible book 1 Kings, chapter 10 and verses 4 to 13.

32
PAINFUL PARTING

H ave you ever tried to do the splits with your legs? It's painful, isn't it? In the Bible story we're going to look at now, God's special nation was about to do the splits and as you'll soon find out, it was jolly painful for them as well.

Israel's third king (Solomon) had started out really well and put God right at the very centre of things. Putting God first meant the nation prospered in a big way. Israel had gold and silver coming out of its ears (not literally of course) and all the nations around about were amazed at what an awesome king Solomon was.

Not for long. Some people collect stamps and others collect coins but King Solomon, well he collected wives. Before you ask I'll tell you how many he accumulated. Seven hundred. Yes, you heard me right. The king's wives weren't all from Israel so they didn't all worship Solomon's God. They brought with them gods of their own. God was having none of that and decided to put a stop to this wickedness.

God collared a chap called Jeroboam and gave him the heads-up that Solomon's days were numbered and that when the king had left this mortal coil (died) Israel would be divided in two. Jeroboam had fallen on his feet 'cos God said that he could be king of the top half of the divided nation.

Not only that, but it would still be called Israel. Ten of Israel's eleven tribes would form this new northern Israel and the tribe of Judah would be left on its own to form the new southern nation which would be called ... well, it's probably pretty obvious what it would called, isn't it? It was going to be called Judah. How original was that?

Want to know who took hold of the reins of Judah after Solomon's death? Of course you do.

Right, head off to Bible book 1 Kings, chapter 11 and check out verses 41 to 43.

SUMMIT SERMON

Jesus might have only spent around three years of His life on earth teaching people about God but He sure packed a lot of stuff into a short space of time. Soon after Jesus had handpicked His twelve disciples (who would carry things on after He was gone) Jesus got cracking with a spot of no-holds-barred teaching.

Because Jesus was healing the sick left, right and centre and because what He had to say packed a punch, He quickly attracted big crowds. Things might have been hectic but Jesus wanted to spend some one-to-one time with His disciples. He slipped away to a nearby mountain, plonked Himself on the ground and began to tell them some mega-important things about God and God's way of doing things.

Before I tell you what Jesus said, one thing you need to know is that God often does things differently to how we might expect. For instance, God encourages us to be generous with our money and *He'll* ensure we lack nothing. How topsy-turvy is that? You give away and you end up with everything you need. Or if someone nicks your coat, God's advice is to give 'em your shirt as well. Doubly topsy-turvy! It's as if God is saying these things to help His love, generosity and forgiveness to flow through us.

What Jesus had to say on this mountain has become known as 'The Sermon on the Mount' and you can find it in Bible book Matthew, chapter 5. Here's how Jesus kicked it off. 'Happy are those who know they are spiritually poor; the Kingdom of heaven belongs to them!' For your information the kingdom of heaven is simply anywhere that God is allowed to be No.1. If we trust in God 100% we're saying that God is more important to us than anything else and as we do this, God will meet all our needs. How cool is that? Depending on God comes up quite a bit in the Bible.

Take a look at Bible book Proverbs, chapter 3 and verse 5 to see what I mean.

34

TOO BIG FOR YOUR BOOTS!

Let's continue with some of the things that Jesus taught in 'The Sermon on the Mount'. Next up Jesus said something that I guess the disciples didn't see coming. 'Happy are those who mourn; God will comfort them!' What's all that about?

It seems like Jesus is saying that there may be things in life which make us sad but with God's life in us we can experience joy and happiness once again. Then Jesus goes on to tell them that 'Happy are those who are humble; they will receive what God has promised!' Wow! The opposite of being humble is to be proud and all through the Bible you can read about people like that who thought that they knew best and didn't need God. Their pride also made them treat other people with contempt which didn't please God one little bit.

In Bible book Proverbs, chapter 16 and verse 18 it spells out the fate of people who get a bit too big for their boots. 'Pride leads to destruction, and arrogance to downfall.' I wonder if Jesus' disciples said anything while Jesus talked to them or whether their jaws dropped with each new thing their Master said. I mean, what would you think if Jesus said (which He did) that God blesses people who want to obey Him more than they want to eat or drink? Did that mean they were meant to starve so that they could serve God? I don't think so. What it probably means is that if you spend your life doing what you want just to satisfy yourself then you've left no room for God. Put God first (and obey Him) and all the other things you need will be yours.

35
PAYBACK TIME

Have you ever heard the expression 'do unto others as you would have them do to you'? Okay so it sounds a bit old fashioned, but what it means is to treat people in the same way as you'd expect them to treat you. Sounds fair, doesn't it?

Well, that was next on the list in Jesus' 'Sermon on the Mount' pep talk to His disciples. Here's how Jesus put it. 'Happy are those who are merciful to others; God will be merciful to them!' Why is it so important to be merciful (kind and forgiving) to other people? That's easy. God allowed Jesus to take the punishment for all the bad things we do so that we can be His friends. All we have to do is to say a big thank You to Jesus, wave goodbye to pleasing ourselves and make God No.1 in our lives. Do that and Jesus promises to come and live on the inside of us to make God seem very real and to help us live a life that pleases God. How amazing is that?

So imagine how God would feel if someone had received His mercy and forgiveness and then decided not to give the same to somebody else. If we want God's mercy we've got to pass it on to others. Just to make that point completely clear Jesus once told a parable about this very thing. It went something like this. A king had a servant who owed him a small fortune. There was no way

the servant could repay his master but when he begged for the chance to pay it back the king gave the guy a second chance. No sooner was the servant free than he headed off to find a fellow servant who owed him a teensy weensy sum of money. The man wasn't able to settle his debt so the unmerciful servant had him chucked into prison.

Find out how the story ends in Bible book Matthew, chapter 18 and verses 31 to 35.

36
TOUGH TIME TALK

Have you heard the joke about the man who walks into a shop and announces, 'I'm here to have my eyes tested'? 'Well, that's pretty obvious', said the shopkeeper. 'This is a butcher's. The optician is next door.' Well, I found it funny even if you didn't.

As Jesus continued to talk to His disciples He also had something to say about not being able to see properly. 'Happy are the pure in heart; they will see God!' Have you ever been in a car when the windscreen is covered in dirt and grime? It's really difficult to see where you're going until the driver squirts some water on it and turns the windscreen wipers on to clear the view. That's better! You can see clearly now.

The bad things we do, think and say are like dirt and grime that get between us and God. One reason the grot builds up is because we don't spend enough time with God and spend too much time doing our own thing. Does this mean we'll literally see God? Probably not, but what it does mean is that we'll find it easier to see how He is leading

us and guiding us each and every day. And that's pretty amazing, don't you think?

When we become Christians we get to call God our Father and that makes us His children. Jesus had something to say about how God expects His children to live. 'Happy are those who work for peace; God will call them his children!' That doesn't mean we have to go around 'shushing' everyone to make it quiet and peaceful. It means that we must do our best to get on with other people and not to fall out with them.

Jesus wrapped up His mountainside pep talk to His disciples with a heads-up that being a Christian wasn't always going to be a bed of roses. He also had some really helpful advice what to do when it wasn't.

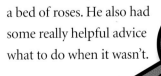

Check this out in Bible book Matthew, chapter 5 and verses 10 to 12.

BIBLE'S GOT TALENT

U nless you've spent the last few years on another planet
(so all you aliens out there can ignore this) you'll have
found it almost impossible to miss at least some of the
TV talent shows that have hit our screens. There seem to be
competitions for just about everything from dancers to dream
jobs; from singers to skaters.

Not to be left out, I figured that it would be a good idea to take
a look in the Bible and to see what talent lies within its pages. In
fact there was so much of it I have decided to call this next bit of
the book, Bible's Got Talent (or BGT; sound familiar?). Novelty
acts always seem to be popular in this type of show, so let's raise
the curtain with a talking donkey, no less. Yep, I'm not kidding.

The donkey's owner (Balaam) was reluctant to do what God
told him, so God decided to grab his attention through the
mouth of his four-legged friend. The donkey wasn't quite so keen
to go against God's wishes, so Balaam beat the stubborn beast
to help it change its mind. That's when God told the donkey to
speak (you can find the story in Bible book Numbers, chapter
22 and verses 22 to 34). 'What have I done to you? Why have you

beaten me these three times? ... Am I not the same donkey on which you have ridden all your life? Have I ever treated you like this before?' Ladies, gentlemen, boys and girls, put your hands together for the talking donkey.

Who's next? Oh yes, it's a ventriloquist act (well, sort of). What, you didn't know there was a ventriloquist in the Bible? In case you're not sure, a ventriloquist is someone who can speak without opening their mouth to make it seem like their puppet is doing the talking. In Bible book Exodus we catch up with a guy called Moses who God was sending to Egypt's Pharaoh to tell him to set his Israelite slaves free. Moses didn't really rate himself when it came to speaking in front of other people and begged God to get somebody else to be His mouthpiece. God wasn't too pleased with Moses' request but eventually went along with his plan.

To find out who opened his mouth for Moses go to Bible book Exodus, chapter 4 and verses 14 to 16.

NOW YOU SEE IT....?

No talent show worth its salt would be complete without a conjurer or two. Trying to work out how they saw their assistants in two (or so it seems) ... without harming them is all part of the fun. And how do they make doves fly from their sleeves or coins simply disappear from their hands before your very eyes? A mystery indeed!

The Bible is full of stories of weird and wonderful things happening that seem to be difficult to explain. They aren't actually conjuring tricks like you might see performed on a talent show but they can still be jaw-droppingly puzzling. For instance, meet Philip. He was a Christian who'd told a man about Jesus, baptised him in a roadside pool of water and had then simply vanished into thin air. Was that magic? Nope, it was God's power taking him away miraculously. For your information Philip ended up in a place called Azotus.

It's not only God who has power in the Bible. God's archenemy, Satan, does as well. Between you and me, Satan wouldn't have any power at all if God hadn't given it to him in the first place. That was when he was on the same side as God but when he rebelled against God he took some of His power with him. Most of the time Satan uses the teensy bit

of power he has to copy what God does, to try and
impress people.

Which brings us on to some real life magicians in the Bible who
tapped into Satan's power to impress the king with their tricks.
God had sent Moses and Aaron to try and convince Egypt's king
(or Pharaoh) to release his Israelite slaves. Hard-hearted Pharaoh
demanded that Moses and Aaron do something miraculous to
convince them that they were sent by God. Aaron rose to the
challenge and threw down his wooden staff (which was sort of
like a walking stick) in front
of Pharaoh and his officials,
and it became a snake.
Wow!

To find out who came centre
stage next to perform their
little magic trick using
Satan's power instead of
God's, read Bible book Exodus,
chapter 7 and verses 8 to 13.

39
DAVID'S DRASTIC DODGE

Time for another act on Bible's Got Talent. Next up we have a guy who rose to fame as Israel's second ever king.

This rags to riches story began with a guy called David looking after his dad's flocks and ended up with him on the throne of Israel's special nation. Not content with ruling the country, King David also makes an appearance in the Bible as a dancer. David was leading a great procession towards Jerusalem when he stripped off his royal robes and began dancing around in his ordinary clothes. His wife (Michal) was well embarrassed and no way was she going to give her jigging hubby a round of applause. God saw things differently because the king was dancing in worship to Him. He gave the dancing David ten out of ten for a great performance. What a talented chappie King David was – but that wasn't the end of it.

David was also a dab hand at playing the harp and we're going to listen in on one of his private performances to King Saul (the king before David). King Saul had made a bit of a mess of things and as a result he'd fallen out of God's good books. Things weren't going well for him and Saul was in a bit of a bad way. The only thing that seemed to help was when David rocked up and strummed his harp for the king. The soothing sounds of David playing calmed the king down, but not on this particular day. King Saul might have been a fan of David's music but he wasn't very happy that the young man was more popular with the Israelites than he was. Grrr! Saul was well jealous.

So it will come as no surprise to you how this musical recital ended.

40

CAPTIVE AUDIENCE

Our next acts in Bible's Got Talent are singers. Put your hands together and give a warm BGT welcome to Paul and Silas. Yaaaaay! But first I'll give you a quick bit of the back story to this duo.

Paul and Silas had been staying in a place called Philippi where the pair had been spending their days telling people about Jesus and performing miracles in God's power. Although plenty of people liked them, not everyone did. Paul and Silas were flung into prison for supposedly encouraging the inhabitants to break the law (which they weren't). After they had been severely flogged, Paul and Silas were thrown into prison and the jailer was commanded to guard them carefully. Just to be safe he put them in the inner cell and fastened their feet in the stocks. Sounds a bit rough when you haven't done anything wrong. Were the imprisoned pair peeved? No way! About midnight, just when you'd be thinking about putting your head down and trying to grab some sleep, Paul and Silas began praying and singing hymns. With the other prisoners listening in they sang their hearts out to God.

The Bible doesn't tell us what their captive audience thought of their efforts but it was pretty clear that God was pleased.

Suddenly, there was a mahoosive earthquake and the whole prison shook to its foundations. All the doors swung wide open and everyone's chains came loose. The jailer woke with a start and came running to see what all the commotion was. When he saw that the doors were open he put two and two together and figured (wrongly) that all the prisoners had done a runner. If that was the case he'd be for the chop. He was just about to kill himself with his sword, because of this, when Paul managed to stop him.

Want to find out how the curtain closed on Paul and Silas' big night?

Check out Bible book Acts, chapter 16 and verses 29 to 34.

41
BATTLE OF THE BANDS

Right, it's battle of the bands time and the Bible has a few contenders who are going to fight it out for this section of our Bible's Got Talent show. You'll need to be patient with our first band because they might take a little while to set up.

A whopping two hundred and eighty-eight musicians make up this act and King David has them neatly divided into twelve groups of twenty-four according to the family they belong to. These guys are the musicians from Jerusalem's temple and they were handpicked by Israel's king (David). In fact there are so many of them that it's more like an orchestra, and they don't have just one person in charge (like a conductor) but three. They are Asaph, Heman, and Jeduthun.

If you're wondering what sort of instruments this band played, let me tell you. As well as a bunch of singers, there were harps, stringed instruments and noisy cymbals. The Bible tells us that these guys were tip-top musicians so I think we can expect a great performance, don't you?

Who's next? Looks like those temple guys have a bit of competition from none other than Moses' sister and the

Israelite ladies with their tambourines. The Bible doesn't say how big their group was but they were part of the Israelite convoy who'd just escaped from slavery in Egypt. That's the reason why Miriam and her backing singers were letting rip at the tops of their voices in the first place. They were free at last and simply couldn't keep their happiness in. What a fantastic sound they must have made as they bellowed out their praises to God, with their tambourines adding to the sound.

I WONDER IF GIRL BANDS WILL CATCH ON!

To download the lyrics to Miriam's song head for Bible book Exodus, chapter 15 and verse 21.

42 JUGGLERS

Our last acts in this Bible talent show are a bit of a mixture. For starters, we've got some jugglers (well sort of). This juggling act features none other than the twelve leaders of the world's first church in Jerusalem. Yep, you heard me right. But these guys didn't juggle balls or anything like that. They juggled the day-to-day running of the church. (Okay, so I did say that it was 'sort of' juggling.)

This diligent dozen had ended up doing everything from preaching to making sure the poor among them were fed. At this rate they'd be run ragged and good for nothing. A church meeting was called and seven godly guys were picked to oversee the day-to-day running of the church. And that was the end of their juggling.

Some talent shows feature escapologists who are bound with ropes and padlocks and who then miraculously free themselves before your very eyes. The Bible has its very own escapologist called Peter. He was one of Jesus' disciples and Peter eventually became one of the leaders of the world's first church. The church grew rapidly but not everyone was happy about this. Herod (who ruled the region) wasn't too happy about Peter and Co. spouting off about how wonderful Jesus was, so he had Peter arrested and flung into prison. It seemed like there was no escape for Peter. He was sleeping between two soldiers, bound with two chains, and sentries stood guard at the entrance.

That's what you think! Ladies and gentlemen, boys and girls, prepare to be astounded by Peter the escapologist.

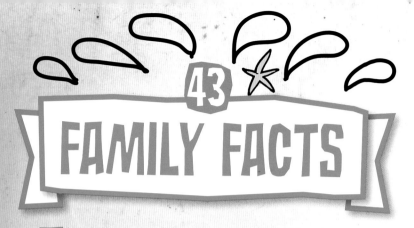

43 FAMILY FACTS

There's an old saying which goes, 'you can't see the wood for the trees'. It means that you can be so close to something that you don't see the bigger picture. That's a bit what it was like for Jesus' brothers and sisters.

What, you didn't know He had any siblings? (That's another word for brothers or sisters.) You bet He did! In fact Jesus had four brothers and at least two sisters. The Bible helpfully gives us the names of the lads (James, Joseph, Simon, and Judas) but has nothing to say about who His sisters were. So there could have been two of them or there could have been more. We'll just never know. To be completely accurate these brothers and sisters were actually half-brothers and sisters and I'll tell you why.

If you know anything about the Christmas story and the birth of Jesus you'll know that it was God who made Jesus' mum pregnant (and not Jesus' human dad, Joseph). God in heaven was Jesus' real Father but Joseph took on the job of being His dad on earth. How's that for team work! The rest of the kids were all from Mary and Joseph so that made Jesus their half-brother.

The Bible makes it clear that Mary and Joseph knew that Jesus was special and had been sent by God but did His

brothers and sisters? We can't be completely certain. Okay, so He must have seemed different to other kids because the Bible tells us that Jesus never did anything wrong. And when Jesus was twelve His parents found Him (after losing Him for three days) in Jerusalem's temple, listening to the teachers and asking them questions. Everyone who heard Him was surprised at how much the youngster knew and at the answers He gave.

The biggest clue to whether Jesus' brothers and sisters understood His true identity was when He hit the road at the age of thirty to begin telling people about God and healing the sick.

Find out what Jesus' family thought about the fuss He was attracting in Bible book Mark, chapter 3 and verses 20 to 21.

44
SIBLING QUIBBLING

The previous Bible bit we looked at was all about Jesus' siblings (his brothers and sisters). Because the Bible has loads of stories about families I figured we could check out a few more.

We used to play the card game Happy Families when our kids were little but we had to stop because our son used to get upset when he didn't win. A game of Happy Families soon became a game of un-Happy Families. It was a bit like that in some of the Bible stories about families. Even the world's first two brothers fell out with each other. Well, to be fair, the eldest son (Cain) was to blame. He was jealous of his kid brother (Abel) and killed him. Not the best sibling story to feature at the beginning of the Bible.

Moving on a few years we come to Joseph. Most people seem to have heard of this young guy because of his 'technicolor dreamcoat' (the Bible actually describes it as a fancy or multi-coloured coat). Not only was Joseph the apple of his dad's eye but God also had His eye on him for a special job. This really riled Joseph's brothers (eleven in all) so they sold him into slavery (in Egypt) and hoped that they'd seen the last of him.

Fear not! In his story there's a happy ending. Joseph ended up as one of Egypt's rulers and was finally reunited with his brothers.

Check it out in Bible book Genesis, chapter 45 and verses 1 through to 11.

45 FAMILY FORTUNES

None of us gets to choose the family we are born into but a guy from the Bible called Moses got a second crack of the whip. He'd been born into an Israelite family and I'll bet his mum and dad loved him very much. The downside was that the Israelites were slaves in Egypt which meant that life was very tough for them.

Just when it seemed that things couldn't get much worse, Egypt's Pharaoh gave an order for all Israelite baby boys to be killed by throwing them into the River Nile. He was worried that if the Israelite population kept on growing at the same rate there'd be a danger of the slaves rising up and overthrowing the Egyptians. Moses' mum hid her little boy (out of harm's way) until he was three months old and then placed him in a basket in the river. The long and the short of it was that Moses was found by Pharaoh's daughter and taken back to the palace to become part of Egypt's royal family. How jammy is that?

But not everyone in the Bible was quite so fortunate with the family they landed up in. When a chap called Achan disobeyed God it wasn't only him who took it in the neck. His family did as well. Here's how it happened. The Israelites had just conquered the city of Jericho but God had warned them not to nick any of the booty for themselves.

Achan was a naughty fella and sneakily snatched a rather nice Babylonian robe, two hundred pieces of silver and a gold bar that weighed the same as fifty pieces of gold. Then he dug a hole under his tent and hid the lot. When the Israelites went to attack the next city on their hit list (Ai) they were defeated big time. God gave Israel's leader (Joshua) the heads-up that it was all down to someone secretly nabbing some of Jericho's treasure. Sure enough, the spotlight shone on Achan but it wasn't only Achan who took the flack for disobeying God.

46

YOU NAME IT

How many names have you got? I've got three but I don't use my middle name as you can see from the cover of this book. If you're wondering what it is I can tell you that it begins with a 'K', ends in an 'N' and has another three letters in the middle. I'll let you work that one out.

Jesus had more than one name but not in the same sort of way. For starters he was called Jesus which means Saviour, which is pretty handy because that was the job He came from heaven to do. He's also known as Jesus Christ. Christ isn't His surname like Parkes or Patel. Christ was another word for Messiah, which describes a special person sent by God. Why had Jesus been sent by God? I'll tell you.

Our friendship with God had been spoiled by sin (that's all the bad stuff we do). Jesus' mission was to patch things up between us and God, which was good news. But the Bible uses loads of other names to describe Jesus as well and that's where we're headed for in these next few Bible bits.

For starters, Jesus was not only known as the Son of God but He also got tagged the Son of Man. Hang on a minute, Jesus can't be both of those things, can He? Either His Father is God in heaven or He's the son of a human father. So which one is it?

Well, actually it is both, however confusing that might seem. As God's Son, Jesus came down to earth to rescue us. But to do that He had to become human as well, which is why Jesus also needed a human mum and dad. And which is why one of His names was the Son of Man.

Want to find out another name Jesus was given that described Him coming down from heaven to live on earth?

47
A IS FOR ...

The next name of Jesus that we're going to check out could very well boggle your brain, so be warned! In Bible book Revelation (which is the very last book in the Bible) Jesus is called the Alpha and the Omega. Sounds a bit odd, doesn't it? I wonder what it means. Allow me to fill you in.

At around the time the New Testament part of the Bible was written, the Greek language was spoken far and wide, a bit like English is nowadays. People still have their own native languages (like Korean or Croatian) but English is also used when needed. Alpha and Omega were the first and last letters of the Greek alphabet (like A and Z are the first and last letters of ours). In fact it's the first and second letters of the Greek alphabet, Alpha and Beta, which actually form the word alphabet. What a mine of useful information I am.

What the Bible is saying when it calls Jesus the First and the Last is that He was around at the beginning of all things and He'll be around at the very end.

Although Jesus lived on earth for around thirty-three years that wasn't when His story begins. The Bible tells us that it was, in fact, through Jesus that the world (and the universe) were created, right at the very start. To save your fingers having to flick through the Bible I'll tell you what it says in Bible book Colossians, chapter 1 and verses 15 and 16. 'Christ is the visible likeness of the invisible God. He is the firstborn Son, superior to all created things. For through him God created everything in heaven and on earth, the seen and the unseen things, including spiritual powers, lords, rulers, and authorities. God created the whole universe through him and for him.'

Now check out Bible book John, chapter 1 and verses 1 to 4 to see a link between this Bible bit and our next one. Off you go!

48
LIGHTEN UP!

I f you've been going through this book from front to back you'll have read the previous Bible bit before you got to this one. If you haven't, can I suggest you do so now.

Right, here's the link between them. Not only does it talk about Jesus being around right at the very beginning and God creating everything through Him but it gives Jesus another name as well. It calls Jesus the Word. Let's have a think about what that might mean.

We know from the Bible that God created the whole universe by commanding it to come into existence. Here's what it says in Bible book Genesis, chapter 1 and verse 3. 'God commanded, "Let there be light"' and guess what? Light started shining. We can see from this that when God wants something to happen He speaks it into being. So when God wanted to tell the world that He still loved us, He communicated it through Jesus. It was as if Jesus was a living message (or word) from God and that's why He was called the Word. How cool is that?

Time for another name of Jesus. Seeing as we've been looking at how God created light at the beginning of time, how about we look at Jesus as Light of the World? If you're into energy

efficiency then having Jesus as the world's most powerful light source sounds a fantastic idea, but that's not what it means.

When Jesus came to earth 2000-ish years ago the world was a dark place – not because they'd run out of candles, but because most people had turned their backs on God. Although people might have pretended that they were happy, deep down inside of them there was a gloominess that nothing could shift. Jesus had rocked up to turn the lights back on in people's lives by reconnecting us to the source of all life, which is God.

Want to find out whom Jesus handed over the responsibility of keeping this light burning to when He returned to heaven?

All is revealed in Bible book Matthew, chapter 5 and verse 14.

49
GOOD AND BAA-D

In some countries people are often known by the job they do. The Welsh are famous for this. Particularly in the olden days, you might well come across Jones the Butcher or Williams the Baker. People had names that reflected everyday life.

Jesus was no exception. In His day many people made their living from the countryside either growing crops or tending animals. That's why the Bible has loads of stories about shepherds and sheep. They were almost everywhere. When Jesus said that He was the Good Shepherd people would have understood what He meant. A good shepherd looked after his sheep and protected them from danger. When the sheep needed feeding the shepherd would lead them to a place where they could graze and feed themselves to their hearts' content. If one of his flock wandered off, the shepherd would go off to find them. When Jesus called Himself the Good Shepherd He was also saying that there were bad shepherds around, so beware!

But why did Jesus describe Himself in this way? Because He wants to care for us and to look after us in the same way that a real life shepherd might look after his sheep. In fact Jesus even calls people who follow Him his sheep just to get the point across.

Keeping on the sheep theme, another of Jesus' names was Lamb of God. All through the Old Testament part of the Bible the Israelite nation made sacrifices to God to say sorry for the wrong things they'd done and often as not a lamb would be sacrificed. These sacrifices didn't get rid of the wrong things, they just kept the Israelites in God's good books for the time being. They were God's way of showing us that a once-and-for-all sacrifice was needed to do the job properly and guess who that sacrifice would be? Yep, you're right! It was Jesus.

Want to discover the first person to cotton on to who Jesus was?

50
NO.1 NAME

You may be surprised to know that there are over two hundred names for Jesus (or descriptions of Him) in the Bible. Well, that's what someone has worked out who has more time on their hands to count them than I do. If we looked at each and every single one of them this book would have to be ginormous. Because there's a limit to the number of pages we can squeeze in between the covers then this'll have to be our last one. Boo hoo!

We've already found out that Jesus was called the Lamb of God, which meant Him giving up His life as a sacrifice for us. If you know a thing or two about Jesus then you'll probably also know that His life on earth ended when He was crucified on a wooden cross. As far as Jesus' enemies were concerned, they'd seen the last of Him.

What they hadn't bargained on was that Jesus was also the Son of God which meant that they might have killed His body but they couldn't destroy God. Just to prove it, Jesus' Father in heaven brought His one and only Son back to life again and then, after forty days, Jesus returned to heaven. Another description for Jesus was as a Suffering Servant because that's how He ended His life on earth. But when Jesus got back in

heaven there was another name waiting for Him. Sitting on
His throne in heaven Jesus was now described as the King
of kings and the Lord of lords. This name wasn't only for
God's benefit; it was for ours as well. When we give Jesus the
No.1 place in our lives we're saying that Jesus is not only our
Saviour but He's also Lord (or King) of our lives as well.

Will everyone call Jesus their
King or their Lord? Well, not
for now, but one day everyone will.

See what I mean
in Bible book
Philippians, chapter 2
and verses 6 to 11.

NATIONAL DISTRIBUTORS

UK: (and countries not listed below)
CWR, Waverley Abbey House, Waverley Lane, Farnham, Surrey GU9 8EP.
Tel: (01252) 784700 Outside UK (44) 1252 784700 Email: mail@cwr.org.uk

AUSTRALIA: KI Entertainment, Unit 21 317-321 Woodpark Road, Smithfield,
New South Wales 2164. Tel: 1 800 850 777 Fax: 02 9604 3699
Email: sales@kientertainment.com.au

CANADA: David C Cook Distribution Canada, PO Box 98, 55 Woodslee Avenue,
Paris, Ontario N3L 3E5. Tel: 1800 263 2664 Email: sandi.swanson@davidccook.ca

GHANA: Challenge Enterprises of Ghana, PO Box 5723, Accra.
Tel: (021) 222437/223249 Fax: (021) 226227 Email: ceg@africaonline.com.gh

HONG KONG: Cross Communications Ltd, 1/F, 562A Nathan Road, Kowloon.
Tel: 2780 1188 Fax: 2770 6229 Email: cross@crosshk.com

INDIA: Crystal Communications, 10-3-18/4/1, East Marredpalli, Secunderabad –
500026, Andhra Pradesh. Tel/Fax: (040) 27737145
Email: crystal_edwj@rediffmail.com

KENYA: Keswick Books and Gifts Ltd, PO Box 10242-00400, Nairobi.
Tel: (020) 2226047/312639 Email: sales.keswick@africaonline.co.ke

MALAYSIA: Canaanland, No. 25 Jalan PJU 1A/41B, NZX Commercial Centre,
Ara Jaya, 47301 Petaling Jaya, Selangor. Tel: (03) 7885 0540/1/2 Fax: (03) 7885 0545
Email: info@canaanland.com.my

Salvation Publishing & Distribution Sdn Bhd, 23 Jalan SS 2/64, 47300 Petaling Jaya,
Selangor. Tel: (03) 78766411/78766797 Fax: (03) 78757066/78756360
Email: info@salvationbookcentre.com

NEW ZEALAND: KI Entertainment, Unit 21 317-321 Woodpark Road, Smithfield,
New South Wales 2164, Australia. Tel: 0 800 850 777 Fax: +612 9604 3699
Email: sales@kientertainment.com.au

NIGERIA: FBFM, Helen Baugh House, 96 St Finbarr's College Road, Akoka, Lagos.
Tel: (01) 7747429/4700218/825775/827264 Email: fbfm_1@yahoo.com

PHILIPPINES: OMF Literature Inc, 776 Boni Avenue, Mandaluyong City.
Tel: (02) 531 2183 Fax: (02) 531 1960 Email: gloadlaon@omflit.com

SINGAPORE: Alby Commercial Enterprises Pte Ltd, 95 Kallang Avenue #04-00,
AIS Industrial Building, 339420. Tel: (65) 629 27238 Fax: (65) 629 27235
Email: marketing@alby.com.sg

SRI LANKA: Christombu Publications (Pvt) Ltd, Bartleet House, 65 Braybrooke
Place, Colombo 2. Tel: (9411) 2421073/2447665 Email: dhanad@bartleet.com

USA: David C Cook Distribution Canada, PO Box 98, 55 Woodslee Avenue, Paris,
Ontario N3L 3E5, Canada. Tel: 1800 263 2664 Email: sandi.swanson@davidccook.ca

CWR is a Registered Charity – Number 294387

CWR is a Limited Company registered in England – Registration Number 1990308

More of Andy Robb's colourful Bible stories with crazy cartoons and cliff-hanger endings

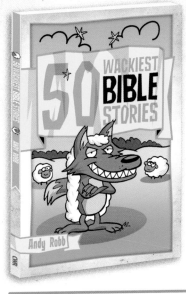

50 Wackiest Bible Stories

Read about some odd methods of transport, odd ways of doing things, the pick of Bible proverbs, lots of Bible double acts and some of Jesus' teaching that has made its way into everyday sayings. Andy Robb, author of the *Professor Bumblebrain* series, has collected together some of the wackiest passages of Scripture in *50 Wackiest Bible Stories*. Andy's witty and conversational style plus colourful illustrations brings God's Word to life for children.

ISBN: 978-1-85345-983-2

50 Jammiest Bible Stories
ISBN:
978-1-85345-851-4

50 Barmiest Bible Stories
ISBN:
978-1-85345-852-1

50 Goriest Bible Stories
ISBN:
978-1-85345-530-8

50 Weirdest Bible Stories
ISBN:
978-1-85345-489-9

50 Wildest Bible Stories
ISBN:
978-1-85345-529-2

50 Craziest Bible Stories
ISBN:
978-1-85345-490-5

For current prices visit www.cwr.org.uk

MORE FROM ANDY ROBB

Professor Bumblebrain offers some exciting explanations, colourful cartoons and (ahem) 'hilarious' jokes answering these important questions:

Who is God? What is He like? Where does He live? How can I get to know Him?
ISBN: 978-1-85345-579-7

Who's the bravest? Who's the funniest? Who's the jammiest? Who's the strongest?
ISBN: 978-1-85345-578-0

Who is Jesus? Where did He come from? What was His mission? What's it to me?
ISBN: 978-1-85345-623-7

Who made the universe? How old is planet Earth? What about dinosaurs? Was there really a worldwide flood?
ISBN: 978-1-85345-622-0

Learn about the meaning behind The Prodigal Son, The Wise and Foolish Man, The Lost Sheep and many more!
ISBN: 978-1-85345-947-4

What is prayer? How can we use it? Does it work? Who in the Bible used it?
ISBN: 978-1-85345-948-1

Get into God's Word

Topz is a popular bimonthly devotional for 7- to 11-year-olds.

The Topz Gang teach biblical truths through daily Bible readings, word games, puzzles, riddles, cartoons, competitions and simple prayers.

Available as an annual subscription (6 bimonthly issues includes p&p) or as single issues (excludes p&p).

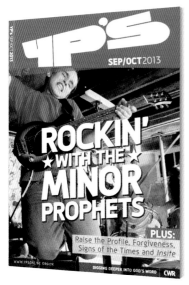

YP's is a dynamic bimonthly devotional for 11- to 15-year-olds.

Each issue is packed with cool graphics, special features and articles, plus daily Bible readings and notes for two months.

Available as an annual subscription (6 bimonthly issues includes p&p) or as single issues (excludes p&p).

For current prices visit **www.cwr.org.uk**
Available online or from Christian bookshops.

Topz SECRET STORIES

from Alexa Tewkesbury

The Topz Secret Stories are full of fun as the rival Dixons gang present problems and opportunities to the Topz gang. They help you to discover things about yourself and God.

Danny and the Runaway
ISBN: 978-1-85345-991-7

The Cloudgate Mystery
ISBN: 978-1-85345-992-4

One Too Many For Benny
ISBN: 978-1-85345-915-3

Pantomime Pandemonium
ISBN: 978-1-85345-916-0

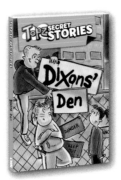

Dixons' Den
ISBN: 978-1-85345-690-9

Dixons and the Wolf
ISBN: 978-1-85345-691-6

For current prices, visit **www.cwr.org.uk/store**
Available online or from Christian bookshops.